National Trust
Inspirational Gardens
Through the Seasons

Foreword by Rachel de Thame

National Trust
Inspirational Gardens
Through the Seasons

Helene Gammack

First published in the United Kingdom in 2014 by
National Trust Books
1 Gower Street
London WC1E 6HD

An imprint of Pavilion Books Company Ltd

ISBN 9781909881204

A CIP catalogue record for this book is available from the British Library.

20 19 18 17 16 15 14
10 9 8 7 6 5 4 3 2 1

Design by Lee-May Lim
Reproduction by Mission, Hong Kong
Printed and bound by 1010 Printing International Ltd., China

This book can be ordered direct from the publisher at the website
www.pavilionbooks.com, or try your local bookshop. Also available at
National Trust shops and shop.nationaltrust.org.uk.

PREVIOUS PAGE Herbaceous borders at Dyffryn Gardens, Glamorgan,
in July. A grass path leads you on to a seat at the end. **LEFT** Poppies in the
Walled Garden at Hinton Ampner, Hampshire, in July. **RIGHT** The purple
border at Sissinghurst contains cottage garden favourites, including lupins
and purple cranesbill.

Contents

foreword

Britain's National Trust gardens, large and small, could be described as a tapestry of riches, each with its own distinctive atmosphere and character. I have been visiting them since childhood with my family, and am fortunate to have seen many more during the course of my work filming across the length and breadth of the country. Some are among the best-known gardens anywhere in the world, and my early outings to the quintessentially English 'garden rooms' at Hidcote, Vita Sackville-West's masterpiece at Sissinghurst, and the verdant lawns and classical temples at Stowe, were formative in making me want to pursue a career within horticulture.

One never tires of revisiting gardens of this quality. For me the greatest pleasure is to be had from returning at different times of year. Each visit offers a different perspective and the chance to see a much-loved garden afresh. I look forward to winter, which brings another opportunity to go back to Anglesey Abbey when drifts of snowdrops carpet the ground, and I always rather hope it might start pouring when I go to Fountains Abbey and Studley Royal during autumn, so I can watch the still pools becoming animated as raindrops hit the surface of the water, shaking up the rich bronze, gold and vermillion hues of the reflected trees. Here, and at Ham House near Richmond in Surrey, I'm reminded how effectively the structured evergreen hedges, topiary and parterres, architectural elements and statuary can define a landscape in every season, and, by contrasting with nature's haphazard beauty, enhance it further.

Each visit is a building block in a lifetime of experiencing gardens. We become the sum of every garden we see and all the plants we touch, smell and tend. Every time I turn up at one of the National Trust gardens, I'm primed and ready to be wowed by sweeping vistas and carefully considered focal points. But it's equally pleasurable to take time to notice the smallest changes as one season blurs into the next: the swelling buds on bare stems as winter gives way to spring, translucent leaves unfurling like a butterfly's wing at the beginning of the growing season, and the indefinable but unmistakable tipping point when a flower slips from being fully open to going over, just as summer morphs quietly into autumn.

This book is a celebration of the seasonal merry-go-round. Our equitable climate enables us to grow a vast selection of plants, giving British gardens incredible depth and range. Nowhere is this more apparent than in the gardens of the National Trust. That we are all able to visit and enjoy them throughout the year is an absolute joy.

Rachel de Thame

2014

LEFT The gardens in July at Sissinghurst Castle, Kent. Sissinghurst achieved international fame in the 1930s when Vita Sackville-West and Harold Nicolson created a garden there.

introduction

This book will take you on a sublime journey, from the anticipation and excitement of spring, as buds and bulbs burst forth, to summer's sumptuous sun-drenched borders, the experience of wading through a garden's leafy autumn blanket and, finally, an appreciation of the stark beauty of winter. Beautifully illustrated and full of vivid descriptions, it is a cornucopia of horticultural feasts for the eye and the mind, in every season and at every turn.

Chapters on spring, summer, autumn and winter showcase the best that there is to see in National Trust gardens through the seasons. You will also find examples of water in garden design,

the now fashionable grasses, summer meadows and orchards, and the contributions that formality and statuary make to seasonal views. There are tantalizing descriptions and images of some of the best plants for each season or situation, which will inspire you to create stunning combinations in your own garden.

The real stars in gardens are, of course, the plants; the way that they are arranged is where the National Trust truly has something exceptional to offer the garden visitor, no matter what the season. Our gardens are home to a vast collection of special as well as common plants and nowhere else will you find such botanical richness and diversity. The fact that National Trust gardens can grow such a wide range of plants is down to our equitable climate and our long history. Our gardens are distributed across the UK and thrive in many different growing conditions. Britain's global activities down the centuries provided access to new continents and vast ranges of plants. Exciting new plant discoveries were brought back to these shores by some of the most famous plant hunters and explorers of their times. The results of their efforts can be seen today, in their full maturity.

But plants alone do not make up a garden. So enjoying a year in a garden is also about enjoying its design, layout or structure. These pages provide a glimpse into the widely varying styles and characters of National Trust gardens, each special in its own right, each providing an example of different approaches to laying out gardens over the centuries.

Seasonal interest in gardens, of course, also includes the benefits of eating some of nature's bounty. This is where kitchen gardens come into their own. After a period of decline in the early twentieth century, many of these beautiful walled gardens have been restored and traditional skills resurrected. Volunteers, such as the 50-strong group on the Wimpole Estate in Cambridgeshire, have enabled the National Trust to bring them back to life and, in many instances, the catering operations provide visitors with an opportunity to literally 'taste the past' throughout the growing season. Produce includes apple varieties that go back hundreds of years, unusual vegetables grown from heritage seed and fruits grown under glass, such as early strawberries, grapes, figs, apricots and citrus fruits.

ABOVE RIGHT Mottisfont's Rose Garden in June. RIGHT A giant snowdrop in the Winter Garden at Anglesey Abbey, Cambridgeshire. OPPOSITE Shades of autumn envelope the Palladian Bridge at Stowe, Buckinghamshire. There are only three other bridges of this style in the country: the other two are at Prior Park Landscape Garden in Somerset and Wilton House in Wiltshire. The identity of the architect is uncertain, but it was probably built under the direction of James Gibbs.

Gardens are constantly changing, whether through seasonal cycles and fluctuating weather patterns, or in response to new trends and fashions. Although the National Trust is guardian to gardens of historic interest, there is room to incorporate new ideas and developments, such as the new herbaceous borders at Packwood House in Warwickshire (see page 84), and the modern sculpture at Antony in Cornwall (see page 125).

Watching subtle changes from week to week, sometimes even day to day, is the inherent joy of being in a garden. This is why more and more gardens are opening all year round. In the depths of winter, some gardens have exceptional displays of bark, flowers, foliage and one of the most exciting winter treats for the senses – scent. Some properties, such as Anglesey Abbey (see pages 200–209), Dunham Massey and Mottisfont, have whole areas designed as winter gardens, where the best winter-performing plants have been arranged together in dramatic compositions.

No matter what the season, there is always something inspiring and new to see in National Trust gardens. So, this is a book which deserves to be on every garden lover's shelf; you can come back to it time and again, whether to re-live the joys of summer when sitting in front of a winter fire, or to dip into for fresh ideas for improving your own garden. Our thanks should go to the National Trust's talented gardeners and volunteers, who make this all possible.

Mike Calnan

Head of Gardens
2014

LEFT The majestic Palladian Bridge at Prior Park Landscape Garden, Somerset. Architectural structures add year-round interest to any garden (see pages 216–227).

spring

Spring Gardens

The longer days and warming temperatures of spring herald an awakening in country estates and gardens. Woodland vegetation is the first to take advantage of the increasing sunlight, before the trees above it are clothed in new leaves and cast their summer shade. The first bulbs to emerge from hibernation are snowdrops, which carpet the naked woods, closely followed by a succession of spring flowers. Wood anemones continue the white theme in early spring, while further on in the season (and prolific in parts of the West Country), great swathes of wild garlic appear. From a distance these look like a late snowfall, only their pungent odour giving the game away.

Bright yellow daffodils reflect the optimism of spring. The native species is at home in rough grass, where the leaves can die back discreetly when flowering is over. Snake's head fritillaries naturalise well in damp meadows, their chequered heads nodding just above the grass, while dog's tooth violets prefer short grass, particularly around deciduous trees.

Crocuses, while short in stature, flower early enough to compete with the grass. The woodland crocus flowers first and spreads very quickly. At Lacock Abbey in Wiltshire, crocuses have naturalised to form a sea-blue carpet in the arboretum (see pages 20–21).

PREVIOUS PAGE A heady spring-flowering ornamental cherry in full bloom in the Walled Garden at Nymans, West Sussex. RIGHT In spring, Prior Park Landscape Garden in Bath, Somerset, is clothed in vast expanses of the distinctive snowy white flowers of wild garlic, a seasonal contrast to the otherwise green and tranquil landscape.

LEFT The daffodils naturalised in the orchard at Sizergh Castle, Cumbria, produce a golden glow. **ABOVE LEFT** A chequered snake's head fritillary flowering at Hinton Ampner, Hampshire. **ABOVE RIGHT** Bright yellow erythronium flowers at Powis Castle, Powys. **BOTTOM LEFT** The starry flowers of wild garlic at Dunster Castle in Somerset. Its pungent leaves add delicious flavours to springtime soups. **BOTTOM RIGHT** The parrot tulip 'Estella Rijnveld', reminiscent of the flowers depicted in Dutch still-life paintings – suitably planted in the Dutch-style formal garden at Hanbury Hall in Worcestershire.

LEFT Naturalised blue and white
crocuses carpet the ground at
Lacock Abbey, Wiltshire.

21

Violets, primroses and cowslips are much-loved natives of woodland clearings but are equally happy in the garden, self-seeding in unexpected places such as crevices in walls and cracks in paving, where little else will flourish. An orchard provides a natural showcase for many of these spring flowers, as they will happily colonise uncultivated ground around trees and complement the abundant, if fleeting, display of pale pink and white blossom on the fruit trees.

Asiatic candelabra primulas provide a more exotic display, flowering from late spring through to early summer. Happiest in a bog garden, they add a dash of colour to the newly emerging fresh green foliage of hostas and ferns. Their pink and orange hues mirror those of their shrubby Asian counterparts, rhododendrons and azaleas, which also flower in late spring.

Other springtime exotics, such as magnolias and camellias, are furnished with a softer palette of white and pink flowers. For sheer glamour, however, it is hard to beat the cascades of beautiful blue wisteria as it drapes itself around buildings or trees, nowhere more beguilingly than at Barrington Court in Somerset, where its abundant long blue racemes tumble over a garden wall down towards the moat (see page 33).

ABOVE Primroses self-seeded in the moss-covered stone walls at Godolphin, Cornwall. RIGHT A swathe of scented old pheasant's eye narcissus flowering in the orchard at Acorn Bank, Cumbria. These emerge in late spring as the early daffodil varieties begin to die down.

FAR LEFT A poppy anemone of the 'De Caen' group growing in the kitchen garden at Ham House and Garden, Surrey. It not only looks good in the garden, but has long been a favourite cut flower with florists. **ABOVE LEFT** The clear blue flower of a winter windflower at Hinton Ampner, Hampshire. **BOTTOM LEFT** The enduringly popular heartsease at Ham House and Garden, Surrey. **RIGHT** Ranks of erect drumstick primulas stud the gardens at Nymans, West Sussex, with regal purple.

FAR LEFT The white flowers and marbled foliage of erythroniums create an attractive carpet in the Delos Garden at Sissinghurst Castle, Kent. **ABOVE LEFT** The native primrose, here growing at Trengwainton Garden, Cornwall, is one of the most charming and accommodating of all spring flowers. **ABOVE RIGHT** A parrot tulip at Hanbury Hall, Worcestershire. **BOTTOM LEFT** The vivid green flowers of the cyclophyllus hellebore at Sissinghurst Castle, Kent, appear from early spring. On a warm day, it is possible to detect their distinct blackcurrant leaf scent. **BOTTOM RIGHT** Clumps of 'Tête-à-Tête' daffodils at Nymans, West Sussex. Their long, trumpet-shaped cups gleam as their heads nod in the early morning light.

ABOVE The blossoming row of cherry trees in the Cherry
Garden at Upton House, Warwickshire, is a spring highlight.
RIGHT Blossom on a gnarled old apple tree in the restored
walled gardens at Llanerchaeron, Ceredigion.

FAR LEFT The Stream Garden at Trengwainton Garden in Cornwall hosts candelabra primulas, including the yellow-flowered *primula helodoxa*, which glow amongst the fresh young foliage of hostas, irises and ferns. ABOVE LEFT The unfurling fronds of the soft tree fern at Trelissick Garden, Cornwall, resemble giant shuttlecocks. BOTTOM LEFT Young hosta leaves uncurl in the sunlit gardens at Rufford Old Hall, Lancashire.

ABOVE In May a curtain of violet-blue wisteria transforms a simple green wooden door on the Entrance Walk at Trelissick Garden, Cornwall, into a magical entrance. RIGHT A waterfall of wisteria cascades over the garden wall towards the moat at Barrington Court, Somerset.

Bluebell Woods

Bluebell woods are some of the most treasured sights in spring: an ethereal, violet-blue haze appears in late April and early May, with a sweet and heady perfume that assaults the senses. Bluebells are native to most parts of Britain, and as they naturalise best in undisturbed soil, they are a prime indicator of ancient woodland. They require plenty of light to flower, so a wood of deciduous native beech trees provides ideal conditions, coming into leaf only after the bluebells have flowered. The distinctive smooth grey bark of the beech blends harmoniously with the blue woodland carpet. Although bluebells do not thrive in competition with other plants, the male fern is a suitable companion. Its fresh green upright crosiers begin to unfurl just as the bluebells are in flower and will ultimately cover the dying bluebell foliage.

As befits such an enchanting and ancient plant, the bluebell is rich in folklore. In times when forests were regarded as mysterious and dangerous places, legend had it that bluebells rang out to summon fairies to their gatherings, but that any human who heard them would meet a fatal end. As with many myths, there may be a germ of truth in the legend: bluebells are poisonous to humans if eaten. On the other hand, they are rich in nectar and provide valuable food for beneficial insects such as bees, butterflies and hoverflies.

The native British bluebell is not to be confused with the stouter, paler and less perfumed Spanish bluebell, which was introduced into gardens in the late 1600s and favoured because it was easily cultivated. Unfortunately, it is now becoming an increasing threat to native species due to cross-pollination.

RIGHT The emerging green tree foliage provides a bright contrast to the carpet of bluebells at Speke Hall, Merseyside. Follow one of the tranquil woodland walks under the spreading trees and listen out for the hum of the bees giving the bluebells their busy attention.

FAR LEFT A carpet of bluebells creates a haze of violet blue against a dramatic blue sky in the wood at Emmetts Garden, Kent. LEFT Young ferns unfurling in April in the bluebell woods at Godolphin, Cornwall. ABOVE The nodding heads of the bluebell flowers at Lanhydrock, Cornwall, merit a closer look.

Garden Varieties

In a garden setting, wild species have long given way to bolder hybrids, bred over hundreds of years by gardeners who prefer more adaptable and brighter versions of the species. The big, top-heavy and powerfully scented Dutch hyacinths, distant cousins of the dainty bluebell, have a strong impact and are especially popular for seasonal bedding, but perhaps the most popular bedding plant is the tulip. Hundreds of varieties in an endless range of colours, shapes and sizes offer gardeners great choice for enhancing the spring garden. These and other spring plants are equally successful whether regimented formally in bedding schemes, or sprinkled randomly around trees in an informal approach – growing as nature intended.

LEFT A harmonious blend of pink and purple tulips gives a contemporary look to the garden at Hinton Ampner, Hampshire. RIGHT Tulips and forget-me-nots are bedded out on a steep slope at Quarry Bank Mill, Cheshire.

ABOVE April: an early morning mist in the Long Garden at Cliveden, Buckinghamshire, lifts to reveal a sea of blue Dutch hyacinths within the formal parterres, punctuated by the bright green of topiary birds and pillars. LEFT A geometric pattern of bulbs and bedding adorn the great parterre at Waddesdon Manor, Buckinghamshire.

At gardens as diverse as Quarry Bank Mill on the Styal Estate in Cheshire and Cliveden in Buckinghamshire, bedding is used to dramatic effect. For sheer grandeur it is hard to beat the great parterre at Waddesdon Manor in Buckinghamshire, designed by Baron Ferdinand de Rothschild in the nineteenth century as an expression of his mastery over nature. Thousands of colourful bulbs and bedding are grown in the geometric compartments and replaced every season. The rigid formality, reinforced by balustrading and clipped yews, is enlivened by a fountain depicting Pluto and Proserpine at its centre.

For an informal approach, it is hard to beat the Lime Walk at Sissinghurst Castle in Kent, where a subtle palette of spring bulbs is planted in a seemingly random manner. The bright colours typical of many garden hybrids provide an opportunity for bold colour schemes, and in Sissinghurst's Cottage Garden, vibrant red tulips are combined with hot-orange wallflowers – a striking combination that sizzles among the contrasting lime-green euphorbias.

FAR LEFT Red tulips, hot-orange wallflowers and nodding aquilegias in cheerful chorus in the Cottage Garden at Sissinghurst Castle, Kent. **ABOVE** Grape hyacinths, snake's head fritillaries and pasque flowers, with contrasting lime green euphorbias, are planted around the base of the trees in the Lime Walk at Sissinghurst. **LEFT** Pink tulips, blue grape hyacinths and nodding snake's head fritillaries are planted in a naturalistic arrangement, also at Sissinghurst.

The Auricula Theatre

One flower that is too precious to plant out in the garden is the show auricula, a member of the primula family. It is as formal as its cousin the cowslip is natural. It is said that auriculas were first introduced to the UK towards the end of the sixteenth century by Flemish weavers fleeing religious persecution. These fancy little plants were quickly adopted by florists who, over generations, bred them in a quest for perfection, culminating in the rarefied versions we see today. Double-flowered auriculas made an appearance by the mid-seventeenth century and, at four times the price of a single-flowered one, proved highly collectable. However, as with the tulip, it was the striped variety that was the elite of the bunch, one reportedly having been sold for the enormous sum of £20. Such enthusiasm is not hard to understand, since few other flowers can equal auriculas in their range of bewitching colours, from blood reds and velvet blacks to ghostly greens or greys; many are coated with a fine dusting of powder, which enhances their otherworldly appearance.

Not surprisingly, these flowers were frequently represented in seventeenth- and eighteenth-century paintings. Indeed, such was their status that they were traditionally grown individually in little clay pots and displayed in wooden 'theatres', complete with a curtain to protect them from strong sunlight and rain. A rare surviving example of an auricula theatre exists at Calke Abbey in Derbyshire, in which rows of colourful auriculas continue to be paraded throughout April and May.

LEFT The auricula 'theatre' at Calke Abbey, Derbyshire. The shelves display a host of auricula primulas in terracotta pots.
RIGHT Detail showing the variety of auriculas on display.

Exotic Introductions

Rhododendrons

Rhododendrons and azaleas thrive in areas of the country with acid soil, and were considered exotic and highly fashionable by the Victorians in their plant-hunting heyday. Many originate from the mountain ranges of China, Tibet and Burma, and were collected by the great plant hunters of the nineteenth century, including Sir Joseph Hooker, George Forrest, Joseph Rock, Frank Kingdom-Ward and Ernest Wilson: names that live on in the plants. Landowners were especially taken with these flamboyant newcomers as not only did they add a dash of colour to their landscape parks but, being evergreen, doubled up as excellent game cover. These vibrant shrubs have continued to flourish in the British climate and, as one of the most colourful highlights of the late spring garden, are very popular with visitors.

LEFT Bright pink rhododendrons flowering in the North Garden at Emmetts Garden, Kent.

ABOVE Brightly coloured rhododendrons and azaleas make an impact in the Spring Ground at Rowallane Garden, County Down. RIGHT A colourful lakeside display of rhododendrons of every colour in the Rhododendron Ground, otherwise known as the American Garden, at Biddulph Grange Garden, Staffordshire.

ABOVE LEFT Dappled shade allows a flamboyant pale pink rhododendron to glow at Quarry Bank Mill, Cheshire. ABOVE CENTRE Lilac rhododendrons flanking gate piers at Clumber Park, Nottinghamshire. ABOVE RIGHT Rhododendrons planted along a woodland walk at Speke Hall, Merseyside. BOTTOM LEFT Rhododendrons in June at the Temple of Apollo at Stourhead, Wiltshire BOTTOM CENTRE Azaleas in flower in the woodland at Trelissick Garden, Cornwall.

Camellias

Another favourite plant of the Victorians was the camellia, admired for its perfectly shaped blooms of crystal white, pink or coral red offset by shiny, dark, evergreen foliage. Camellias were originally cultivated in glasshouses as they were thought to be tender and in need of protection. This proved not to be the case and consequently they were placed in pots on terraces for optimum display or planted in open ground.

ABOVE A variety of the popular pink camellia flowering abundantly at Antony, Cornwall. **RIGHT** Pale pink camellia in April at Nymans, West Sussex.

Magnolias

The elegant appearance of magnolias makes them the ideal trees for stately gardens, although they can look equally at home in a cottage or suburban garden – a single specimen of one of the hardy and free-flowering Soulangiana magnolias is ideal for taking centre stage in springtime. The goblet-shaped flowers of palest pink or deepest purple are, when in full bloom, unencumbered by foliage, which appears only as the flowers fade. Despite their exotic beauty, magnolias are generally very accommodating and will happily put on a fine show without too much fuss. However, a late frost can turn a tree in full bloom brown overnight.

Magnolias are closely associated with the gardens at Nymans in West Sussex, where many varieties were raised, in particular the lilac-pink 'Leonard Messel' magnolia , named after the great collector of plants who lived there in the early twentieth century.

LEFT The goblet-shaped flowers of a deep pink magnolia in the walled garden at Sissinghurst Castle, Kent. A walled garden, like this, offers ideal conditions for a magnolia, providing shelter from harsh winds and reducing the risk of frost.

LEFT The large, rose-purple sub species of Campbell's magnolia, *Mollicomata* 'Lanarth', at Trengwainton Garden, Cornwall.
ABOVE LEFT The waterlily-flowered 'Anne Rosse' magnolia blooming at Nymans, West Sussex. **ABOVE** The delicate shades of a Campbell's magnolia, also at Trengwainton Garden.
RIGHT Confetti-like petals of an old magnolia tree scattered on a path at Godolphin, Cornwall. The stone wall in the background has alcoves, or beeboles, once a common feature in walled gardens.

LEFT Dainty white flowers garland a star magnolia at Trellisick Garden, Cornwall.
ABOVE A Wilson's magnolia flowering at Stagshaw Gardens, Cumbria.

The shorter star magnolia has, as its name suggests, pure white, star-shaped flowers that glow in the evening light and it is a captivating tree for a small garden.

An alluring group of magnolias that flower a little later has nodding, cup-shaped flowers followed by fleshy red fruits that split to reveal scarlet seeds. The most distinct of these are the Wilson magnolia (shown above) and the Chinese magnolia, both of which have scented white flowers with deep crimson stamens that draw you in for a closer look and to inhale their sweet perfume.

RIGHT Visitors photographing a fine magnolia tree in flower in the Walled Garden at Nymans, West Sussex. **FAR RIGHT** The beautiful pink scented flowers of the 'Leonard Messel' magnolia at Nymans, where it was first discovered as a natural hybrid between two Japanese magnolias.

summer

Summer Gardens

Summer is, for many, a long-awaited season, with the promise of glorious sunshine. Flowers are more plentiful and varied than at any other time of the year. Cottage garden favourites are at their best, and a flamboyant assortment of lupins, delphiniums, peonies and irises is typical of the traditional herbaceous border. The heat of the sun releases the perfume of the most scented plants, never more evident than in a rose garden in full flourish. Aromatic herb gardens offer the perfect haven for bees and butterflies, with a plentiful supply of nectar and pollen; these creatures animate the beds and borders as they enjoy the warmer days.

PREVIOUS PAGE August at Tyntesfield, Somerset: wild flowers are grown in the meadows and also in the kitchen garden to pick for the house. LEFT Exotics in the Italian Garden at Mount Stewart, County Down, with palms and cabbage trees lining the central avenue. ABOVE The purple border in the height of summer at Sissinghurst Castle, Kent: magenta roses under-planted with purple cranesbill.

Summer meadows are also visited by an abundance of wildlife. As a contrast to the well-ordered traditional beds and borders, several National Trust properties are reducing the management of grassy areas for the benefit of wild flowers. The chalky soil at Polesden Lacey in Surrey provides ideal conditions for the poppies and cornflowers that thrive amongst meadow grasses, while at Tyntesfield in Somerset, areas of the lawns are left uncultivated to encourage colonies of wild species.

ABOVE AND BELOW LEFT Wild flowers at Polesden Lacey, Surrey, in July. RIGHT August at Tyntesfield, Somerset: wild flowers are grown in the meadows and also in the kitchen garden to cut for the house.

During the hottest days of summer, a fountain is a refreshing sight, cooling the air and creating a rhythm of splashing water (see page 122). Fountains are particularly well suited to gardens planted with hot-coloured exotic species. At Mount Stewart in County Down, Northern Ireland, water features lend the Italian Garden and the sunken Spanish Garden a strong Mediterranean character.

The long daylight hours of summer provide an opportunity to enjoy the garden late into the evening, an ideal time for unwinding. Strategically placed seats invite you to sit and enjoy the sights and sounds; a pretty bench also serves as an ornamental focal point. Both practical and decorative seats are a reminder of one of the principal purposes of a garden – a place for rest and relaxation.

FAR LEFT Blue phlox flowering on the Orangery Terrace in July at Powis Castle, Powys. The tall white foxgloves in the foreground echo the statue in the distance. **ABOVE LEFT** A circular iron garden seat around a tree in the garden at Red House, Kent. **LEFT** This white bench facing the fountain in the Rose Garden at Emmetts Garden, Kent, is an invitation to stop and enjoy the view and the scents of the garden.

The Herbaceous Border

An herbaceous border in midsummer epitomises the traditional English country garden. In its grandest incarnation it was designed to be in full bloom when estate-owning families spent the summer season in the country. With a typical profile of tall plants at the back, graduating down to the shortest at the front, these borders were traditionally well ordered and generally sheltered by a wall or clipped hedge to provide a dark foil for the colourful blooms. This style dominated for a great part of the twentieth century and was championed by the most influential gardening figures of the day, in particular Gertrude Jekyll, who advocated a colour order of subtle gradations to temper an otherwise mingled appearance. Colour combinations were carefully considered for contrast or harmony, with foliage colour as important as that of the flower.

RIGHT July at Peckover House and Garden, Cambridgeshire: vibrant hot colours sizzle in the red border.

LEFT Yellow daylilies and yarrow combine with orange red hot pokers and blue globe thistles in the borders on the Orangery Terrace in July at Powis Castle, Powys. **ABOVE** Yellow red hot pokers and dahlias are among the hot-coloured flowers in the garden at Killerton, Devon, in August.

LEFT A narrow paved path leads you through billowing, pastel-coloured borders of pink, blue and white flowers in the Rose Garden at Sissinghurst Castle, Kent. **ABOVE** Tall, feathery plumes of white goat's beard combine with a predominantly blue choice of flowers in the large herbaceous border in June at Sizergh Castle, Cumbria. **NEXT PAGE** The impressive curved border in the Herbaceous Garden at Anglesey Abbey, Cambridgeshire, is backed by a formal hedge with towering trees behind. It is comprised of traditional favourites such as delphiniums, peonies and bellflowers united by a ground cover of hardy geraniums.

As an alternative, the enduringly fashionable single-coloured borders focused on texture and form, as represented in the celebrated pair of red borders at Hidcote in Gloucestershire, which employs red and purple foliage together with red flowers to enhance the theme. These double borders, bisected by a path, represent a traditional layout, very popular in the Edwardian period. At Nymans in West Sussex, the Edwardian borders run either side of a gravel path towards an Italian fountain flanked by giant topiaried yews, a pattern echoed in Thomas Mawson's Edwardian design at Dyffryn Gardens in the Vale of Glamorgan, where a grass path leads you on to a seat at one end.

Traditionally, herbaceous borders were predominantly planted with hardy perennials for maximum impact in midsummer. Recently, in line with a less formal style of planting, most borders now supplement the traditional palette with half-hardy perennials (many flowering right up until the first frosts) and longer-flowering annuals, which are encouraged to self-seed. These, together with the inclusion of shrubs and grasses, present a more random profile while extending the season of interest.

RIGHT Red lobelia at Peckover House, Wisbech, Cambridgeshire. The purple foliage is a harmonious foil to the scarlet flowers. **FAR RIGHT** The red borders at Hidcote, Gloucestershire, planted with the daylily `Kwanso Flore Plena', `Queen Victoria' and `Will Scarlet' lobelia, and miscanthus `Gracillimus'.

LEFT The well-ordered and brightly coloured double borders at Nymans, West Sussex in August. The gravel path leads towards a red Verona marble fountain. ABOVE Herbaceous borders at Dyffryn Gardens, near Cardiff in South Glamorgan in July. A grass path leads you on to a seat at the end. In both cases these are formal borders with the plants ranged neatly by height, the smallest ones spilling just a little way over the edge to soften the geometry.

ABOVE AND RIGHT At Packwood House, Warwickshire, contemporary-style herbaceous borders In the Walled Garden are planted with cool blue and white perennials combined with the tall, translucent spires of golden oat grass (above). In June the yellow and purple border sports tall yellow mulleins and blue biennial clary sage.

LEFT Hot yellow yarrows, orange montbretia and sneezeweed combine with succulent dark purple houseleek trees to add a dash of Mediterranean glamour to the Raised Terrace borders at Packwood House, Warwickshire. **ABOVE LEFT** A red poppy at Mottisfont, Hampshire. **ABOVE RIGHT** The metallic blue thistle of a sea holly growing in the gardens at Wallington, Northumberland. **BOTTOM LEFT** An early summer-flowering peony 'Bowl of Beauty' at The Courts Garden, Wiltshire. **BOTTOM RIGHT** The fringed yellow daisy flower of Hooker's inula at Wallington, Northumberland.

LEFT AND ABOVE Red and white forms of valerian in the herbaceous beds in front of Robert Adam's eighteenth-century summer house in the Pleasure Grounds at Osterley Park, Middlesex. This informal style of planting is very much in the modern style and creates a relaxed and natural look.

ABOVE LEFT Purple-flowered dittany in the Rose Garden at Sissinghurst Castle, Kent. It is also known as the burning bush as it produces volatile oils which can ignite in the heat of the summer sun. **ABOVE CENTRE** Zinnia, an annual, partners quaking grass in August at Sizergh Castle, Cumbria. **ABOVE RIGHT** Pale pink alliums in the Australasian Garden at Dyffryn Gardens, Glamorgan, in July. **BOTTOM LEFT** Purple allium flowers at Canons Ashby, Northamptonshire. **BOTTOM CENTRE** A border of alliums at Packwood House, Warwickshire.

LEFT AND ABOVE Examples of cool and hot borders at Powis Castle, Powys, in August. The dramatic, Italianate setting of Powis Castle gives an interesting twist to what is a particularly British way of planting.

ABOVE LEFT The gardens at Great Chalfield Manor, Wiltshire, are studded with graceful columbines. **ABOVE RIGHT** Stately yellow lilies grace the late summer garden at Erddig, Wrexham. **BOTTOM LEFT** California poppies in July at Godolphin, Cornwall. **BOTTOM RIGHT** A brightly coloured gazania flowering in September at Hidcote Manor Garden, Gloucestershire.

ABOVE LEFT Late summer at Hidcote Manor Garden, Gloucestershire, sees the sky-blue spires of Russian sage in flower. This elegant, aromatic plant has chalk-white stems that remain attractive throughout the winter. **ABOVE RIGHT** Pink, red and blue anemones flowering in June at Biddulph Grange Garden, Staffordshire. **BOTTOM LEFT** Red tiger lilies bask in the August sun at Acorn Bank, Cumbria. **BOTTOM RIGHT** Elegant angel's fishing rods get their name because of their thin, wiry stems. Here they are growing on the Main Terrace at Hinton Ampner, Hampshire, in July.

FAR LEFT Robust orange red hot pokers and delicate pink angel's fishing rods are an unusual but beguiling combination when seen in the soft light of a rain-washed summer's day at Coleton Fishacre, Devon. **ABOVE LEFT** Armenian cranesbill in the herbaceous border at Anglesey Abbey, Cambridgeshire. **ABOVE RIGHT** A regal lily on the Main Terrace at Hinton Ampner, Hampshire, in July. **BELOW LEFT** Blue lupins in the Walled Garden at Hinton Ampner in July. **BELOW RIGHT** A foxglove flowering in June at Tintinhull Garden, Somerset.

LEFT The Mediterranean-style herbaceous borders surrounding *First Flight*, a bronze statue by Albert Bruce Joy in the Statue Garden at Overbeck's, Devon. **ABOVE** An eye-catching combination of scarlet montbretia 'Lucifer' with blue and yellow flowers in the garden at Overbeck's.

The Rose Garden

One of the highlights of the summer garden and of the gardening year is the rose garden. The first buds of early summer excite great anticipation as they unfurl to flaunt their midsummer display of voluptuous, fragrant blooms.

Rose gardens have changed according to fashions, available labour and space. The roses of the Victorian era, with tissue-like petals, gave way to the formal, tightly scrolled flowers of the hybrid tea varieties. These, together with polyantha and floribunda roses, were the roses of choice in the first half of the twentieth century. Planted in a border, or typically geometric rose beds, without any competition from other plants, they were a requisite feature of gardens large or small.

LEFT AND BELOW The Rose Garden at Sissinghurst Castle, Kent (left), with a detail of the shrub rose 'Constance Spry' (below).

TOP The hybrid tea rose 'Savoy Hotel' at Peckover House, Cambridgeshire. ABOVE Hybrid tea rose 'Pot o' Gold', also at Peckover House. RIGHT Rose 'Rhapsody in Blue' in the Rose Garden at Lyme Park, Cheshire.

LEFT The moss rose 'William Lobb' at Beningborough Hall, Yorkshire. RIGHT A single-flowered rose, *Rosa glauca*, flowering at Hinton Ampner, Hampshire. Despite its simple form, the plant's bright red hips and blue-grey foliage secure its place in the garden. BELOW A 'Fantin-Latour' rose at Greys Court, Oxfordshire.

At Bateman's in East Sussex, Rudyard Kipling added a Victorian-style rose garden during his tenure (1902–36). It is planted with pink and red varieties of polyantha roses and today, in order to extend the season of interest, it has been under-planted with the small, spring-flowering bulbs of the 'Hawera' daffodil and 'Blue Spike' grape hyacinth.

An unusual, Art Deco-style rose garden of curved and circular beds, originating in the 1920s, still exists at Morden Hall Park in Surrey, where over 2,000 roses flower from May to September. Roses are now more typically planted with herbaceous perennials to complement their colour and form and to extend the flowering season of the garden. Hardy geraniums are especially successful in hiding the often ungainly stems of the rose bush and supressing any potential weed invasion.

LEFT The rose garden at Bateman's, Rudyard Kipling's home in East Sussex.

Traditional herbs also make excellent companions for roses: lavender or catmint is a conventional edging for pathways in a rose garden, the blue flowers and soft grey foliage being a perfect foil for the subtle hues of the roses. Such combinations can be seen at Gunby Hall in Lincolnshire, a rose-lovers' paradise where roses of all forms scramble up dovecotes and over arches, cascade into water and envelop the walls of the handsome William and Mary house, as well as behaving politely in their shrubbery beds. For the keen rosarian, there are rarities to be found here, including the rambler 'Elisa Robichon' and the Victorian climber 'Reine Marie Henriette'. This informal approach also suits the resurgence of a more relaxed and softly coloured style of bloom – the pre-twentieth-century 'old-fashioned' roses.

Mottisfont Abbey in Hampshire is the National Trust's flagship rose garden, designed in 1972 by the eminent rose expert and National Trust gardens advisor Graham Stuart Thomas, who based the formal layout along the lines of the walled kitchen garden in which it is situated. A circular lily pool, created from the original dipping pond, is a central focal point, while pillars of Irish yew and low clipped box edging frame the billowing sprays of roses. Herbaceous planting adds variety of form and colour. More than 40 years later, Mottisfont's Rose Garden remains one of the most sumptuous and sensuous of gardens.

RIGHT Rose beds are edged with lavender in the Pergola Garden at Gunby Hall, Lincolnshire. The walls around this garden create a warm, sheltered area in which the aromas of these lovely flowers linger on sunny summer days.

LEFT A June view in the Rose Garden at Mottisfont in Hampshire. The arches are covered in 'Adélaide d'Orléans' roses and the crisp lines of the box hedges provide structure. **ABOVE** 'Raubritter' roses flowering in June by the side of the fountain pool in the same Rose Garden.

FAR LEFT The National Trust's flagship rose garden at its most abundant in June at Mottisfont, Hampshire. The garden, located in the old walled kitchen garden, was designed in 1972 by Graham Stuart Thomas, the National Trust's first gardens advisor and rose expert. THIS PAGE Roses at Mottisfont (clockwise from top left): the hybrid tea rose 'George Arends'; rose 'Graham Thomas', named in honour of the great rosarian who designed the rose garden; 'Tuscany superb'; *Rosa mundi*, a striped form of the old apothecary's rose.

ABOVE Rose arches in full bloom in the Rose Garden at Nymans, West Sussex.

RIGHT A gravel path is bordered by the catmint 'Six Hills Giant' together with pillars of climbing roses, also at Nymans.

The Herb Garden

Herbs are the perfect all-round plant: ornamental, aromatic and edible. The oils from the green or grey foliage are released in the heat of the sultry summer sun, infiltrating the air with intense perfumes and evoking their Mediterranean origins. The flowers are generally less showy than those of other garden plants but they nevertheless produce generous quantities of intensely coloured blue, yellow or pink spires. Angelica and fennel provide height and their glowing, acid yellow umbels tower above borders, while bay, sage, rosemary and thyme add texture and structure and have the bonus of evergreen foliage. As to flavour, even a small quantity of a fragrant herb can enhance most dishes.

FAR LEFT The well-ordered herb garden in the East Walled Garden at Llanerchaeron, Ceredigion, with fennel in the foreground.
ABOVE LEFT The blue, star-shaped flowers of borage at Barrington Court, Somerset.
ABOVE RIGHT Angelica in the Herb Garden at Greenway, Devon.
BOTTOM LEFT The attractive purple flowers of chives in June, seen in the kitchen garden at Biddulph Grange Garden, Staffordshire.
BOTTOM RIGHT Fennel growing in the kitchen garden in July at Ham House, Surrey.

Several National Trust properties have reinstated herb gardens to complement their historic houses. Some are designed in a formal configuration, while others follow a billowy cottage-garden style, especially when intermingled with roses, irises and peonies, themselves once grown for medicinal purposes. At Hardwick Hall in Derbyshire, one of the largest herb gardens in the country has been created in a scale entirely appropriate to the imposing Elizabethan mansion, with equally suitable plants for the period (see page 116). The Herb Garden at Acorn Bank in Cumbria (see page 117), although designed in 1969, evokes the property's medieval origins and is planted with possibly the widest collection of medicinal and culinary herbs in the north of the country.

ABOVE The Herb Garden at Coughton Court, Warwickshire, in July. It is designed around a diamond patterned, box-edged parterre. **RIGHT** The New Herb Garden at Scotney Castle, Kent, in July. A wellhead forms a centrepiece.

LEFT The Herb Garden at Hardwick Hall, Derbyshire in summer, where a wigwam of golden hops is growing amongst wild leeks, pot marigolds and cotton lavender. **ABOVE** The Herb Garden at Acorn Bank, Cumbria.

The physic beds at Wordsworth House and Garden in Cumbria are comprised of medicinal herbs with charming, self-explanatory names such as self-heal, hedge woundwort and feverfew. Half-standard apples, together with the striped apothecary's rose, *Rosa mundi*, and hedges of lavender provide structure. Reflecting the period when William Wordsworth and his family lived here, the physic garden is as much an academic study in the value of herbs as it is a gardener's delight.

For a very different approach, the personality of the gardener really shines through in the Herb Garden at Sissinghurst Castle in Kent where Vita Sackville-West, together with her husband Harold Nicolson, demonstrated great resourcefulness in their interpretation of a traditional herb garden walled with box hedges. The shallow stone bowl perched on three seated lions (see page 121) overflows in summer with a foam of pink-flowered thyme and provides a focal point to the throne-like seat constructed out of brick and fluted stone, remnants of the Elizabethan building. For comfort, a chamomile cushion is planted on the seat to perfume the air with its apple-like scent, reminiscent of the herb seats in a medieval garden.

LEFT AND ABOVE RIGHT
The Physic Garden at Dyffryn
Gardens, Vale of Glamorgan, in July.
RIGHT Lavender growing in the Pine
Garden at Hidcote, Gloucestershire.

LEFT Lavender and rosemary surround a wooden bench at Wordsworth House and Garden, Cumbria, the birthplace and childhood home of the poet. **ABOVE** A shallow stone bowl overflowing with pink-flowered thyme in the Herb Garden at Sissinghurst Castle, Kent.

Fountains and Water

In the heat of a midsummer's day, no garden is truly complete without the refreshing sight and sound of water. Influenced by the traditional gardens of ancient Persia, water gardens generally took on an axial form as rills, pools and fountains. In Renaissance Italy, water 'jokes' were often hidden throughout gardens, but this development was not wholeheartedly adopted in Britain, where a soaking in our colder climate was unlikely to have been welcomed. Tudor and Stuart gardens employed fountains to show off artistic and mechanical wizardry by creating rainbows and automata, singing birds being a favourite theme.

The most eye-catching fountains incorporate fine sculpture, providing an animated focal point in a garden or park, and the National Trust has a diverse variety in its care. The intricately fashioned figurative marble *Fountain of Love* at Cliveden in Buckinghamshire (see page 124), designed by the Anglo-American sculptor Thomas Waldo Story around 1897, makes a magnificent statement on the approach to the house. By contrast, the pure form of the sculptor William Pye's 3m-high (10ft) water feature at Antony in Cornwall blends seamlessly into the garden. The simple cone echoes the giant cone-shaped yew and the circular roof of the dovecote. It appears motionless, but a closer look reveals a constant flow of water over its smooth bronze surface, either glistening in the sun or with the faintest sheen depending on the time of day, while the gentle sound of water falling into the surrounding reservoir pool is just about audible; altogether a lesson in sublime subtlety.

RIGHT A detail of the Italian marble fountain at Nymans, West Sussex.
FAR RIGHT Sunlight catching the sprays of water from the fountain in the Pond Garden at Lytes Cary Manor, Somerset.

LEFT The exuberant marble *Fountain of Love* by Thomas Waldo Story, c.1897, at Cliveden, Buckinghamshire. **ABOVE** *Anthony Cone* by the contemporary sculptor William Pye on the West Lawn at Antony, Cornwall, could not be more different to Story's flamboyant fountain at Cliveden.

From the medieval period, elaborate sequences of ponds ensured a year-round supply of fish for monasteries and manor houses. The seventeenth-century fashion for all things Dutch led to the transformation of these ponds into formal canals, and Westbury Court in Gloucestershire boasts a rare surviving example (shown left). These in turn gave way to the naturalistic lakes of the eighteenth-century landscape park.

Fountains Abbey and Studley Royal Water Garden in Yorkshire has the finest water gardens in the country, and today is a World Heritage Site. It was created by John Aislabie in the 1720s following his expulsion from government and was inspired by a visit to Italy. The garden contains lakes, grottoes, springs, a long, formal canal, and a round full-moon pond framed by a pair of crescent-shaped ponds (see page 129). These are all set within bowling-green-smooth lawns. Enhancing the water features are architectural adornments including a pair of classical summer pavilions, the Banqueting House and the Octagon Tower. The garden was certainly designed with summer in mind!

All the ponds and lakes that today are appreciated mainly for their mirror-like quality, reflecting the surrounding gardens and parks, would once have been animated either with playful fountains, sailing boats, fish or fowl and were valued as much for their provision of food and entertainment as they were for their ornamental contribution to the garden.

LEFT A rare surviving formal water garden at Westbury Court Garden, Gloucestershire, featuring a canal influenced by the Dutch fashion of the late seventeenth to early eighteenth centuries.

RIGHT A distant view of the Moon Pond and the Temple of Piety at Fountains Abbey and Studley Royal Water Garden, Yorkshire. Although construction of the Moon Pond was begun in 1716, its simple, crisp lines feel remarkably modern in their simplicity. On a sunny summer's day the reflections in the water add subtle interest and enhance the sense of tranquility.

autumn

Autumn Gardens

The most textural of all the seasons, autumn is full of contrasts: brightly coloured late blooms continue to flower amongst the dried carcasses and seed heads of spent perennials, and lush evergreens mingle with deciduous trees and shrubs. Golden sunlight may warm a clear blue sky or break through stormy clouds. At other times, the intensity of the sun is tempered by autumn mists, creating a soft focus on a landscape furnished in rich shades of gold, red and russet, which generate a reassuring warm glow despite the chill of the impending winter. Colour is also to be found in the berries that hang, jewel-like, in the trees and shrubs in bright shades of red and orange, catching the eye of foraging birds. The moisture in the autumn air encourages the emergence of fungi, mushrooms and toadstools, which spring up overnight in grass and woodland, while garlands of fine cobwebs beaded with pearly dewdrops lace the garden.

Despite the exalted beauty of autumn, it is a season tinged with melancholy, as it signifies the end of summer and the drawing to a close of another year.

PREVIOUS PAGE In autumn, an array of colours surrounds the 2-hectare (5-acre) lake at Mount Stewart, County Down. RIGHT Autumn colours in the garden at Powis Castle, Powys.

LEFT A misty autumn light illuminates the transparent petals of pale lemon sunflowers while silhouetting their dried seed heads in the Botanic Garden at Lacock Abbey, Wiltshire.
ABOVE, TOP Stately artichoke seed heads in the soft autumn light at Lacock Abbey.
ABOVE A golden marigold seen through a web of dewy grass on a misty autumn day, also at Lacock Abbey.

ABOVE Mushrooms emerging in autumn at Lyveden New Bield, Northamptonshire. RIGHT The fascinating shape of orange fungi, seen in woodland at Kingston Lacy, Dorset, in October. FAR RIGHT Leaves starting to turn a glowing red in September at Hidcote Manor Garden, Gloucestershire.

Autumn Flowers

The use of annuals and half-hardy perennials in the flower garden guarantees a fine display of colour right up until the first frosts. Seasonal highlights of the autumn border include richly coloured dahlias in assorted shades of yellow, orange, pink and red. Their flower form is almost as varied, ranging from simple flowers on wiry stems to dainty pompoms or stout cactus flowers.

Other late-flowering perennials include daisy-flowered coneflowers (see page 140) and heleniums in fiery colours, and wine-red, fleshy sedums, all of which associate well with the more subdued hues of grasses. As a contrast to the hot colour palette of autumn, starry-flowered asters come in cooler shades – predominantly blue, but also in pinks and whites.

THIS PAGE From left to right, a selection of dahlias for autumn colour: dahlia 'David Howard' at Wallington, Northumberland; dahlia 'Golden Happiness' in the Walled Garden at Clumber Park, Nottinghamshire; dahlia 'Gerry Hoek' growing on the Dahlia Walk at Cragside, Northumberland and the cactus-flowered dahlia 'Doris Day' in the red border at Hidcote Manor Garden, Gloucestershire.

FAR LEFT A border of yellow coneflowers
glows through the fog on an autumn day in
the Botanic Garden at Lacock Abbey, Wiltshire.
ABOVE LEFT Black-eyed Susan in the Kitchen
Garden at Clumber Park, Nottinghamshire.
LEFT White asters flowering in September
at Hidcote, Gloucestershire.

Upton House in Warwickshire holds the National Collection of Asters. It was started in the 1940s by Miss Elizabeth Allen, who, over the following 50 years, established the largest collection in Britain. To ensure its future, a new home was sought where enough space and time could be dedicated to looking after them. The gardens at Upton House fitted the bill and they adopted the collection, which consists of nearly 100 cultivars of Italian aster, heath aster and cordifolius, flowering from September onwards.

Autumn also has a counterpart to the grass and woodland carpeting plants of spring. Colonies of autumn-flowering crocus and cyclamen emerge amongst fallen leaves to inject a rosy pink and purple contrast to the seasonal russet hues, while pools of big blue lilyturf flowers emerge through their dense tufts of grassy evergreen foliage, followed by shiny black berries. The display is a reminder of the regenerative cycle of nature.

LEFT The aster border during Aster Week in September at Upton House, Warwickshire. Upton House is the holder of the National Collection of Asters.
ABOVE Aster 'Jungfrau' has pinkish-purple flower heads with yellow centres, here seen in the aster border at Upton House.

FAR LEFT Clusters of autumn-flowering crocus skirt a tree at Bateman's, East Sussex.

ABOVE Autumn-flowering cyclamen and fallen Japanese maple leaves make a colourful show in November at Woolbeding Gardens, West Sussex.

LEFT The autumn crocus 'Bowles Norfolk' at Felbrigg Hall, Norfolk.

ABOVE The evergreen big blue lilyturf flowering in November at Scotney Castle, Kent.

Grasses

Grasses bridge the transition from summer to autumn; varying little in profile throughout the seasons, they maintain their structure well into winter. They have proved to be an autumn staple, especially when mixed with late-flowering perennials to create a prairie-style planting, an apparently random tapestry of texture and colour. Grasses rely on their form to give structure to a garden, especially in autumn, when many of the herbaceous perennials have exhausted themselves. They move gently in even the softest breeze, which lends animation to a border.

Their colour tends to be subtle, although the most striking have metallic red shots through their leaves or variously textured plumes, most notably in the *Miscanthus* species. Less subtle is the recently much-derided pampas grass, which creates a stately presence when positioned in an appropriate location. Backlit by the autumn sun, few plants can match it for sheer glamour. A group of them rise up majestically from a lawn at Ickworth in Suffolk, fountain-like with feathery plumes and slender sprays of foliage. The pampas grass at Sheffield Park in East Sussex is planted by the edge of a lake, a more natural situation but equally effective (shown left).

The shorter wafts of Mexican feather grass in the borders at The Courts in Wiltshire are interspersed with late-flowering perennials such as stout ruby-red sedum. Behind them, the brilliant orange and scarlet foliage of the stag's horn sumach tree completes the autumn picture. Here, grasses are also used alone to great effect, as beds of the giant golden oat grass are given a dark green backdrop of a yew hedge to show off their elegant structure. Fine spikelets rise up to 2.4m (8ft) high and rustle together as the breeze filters through them. In the new herbaceous borders at Warwickshire's Packwood House, established in 2006, golden oat grass is planted at intervals to give rhythm to the borders and create a shimmering, translucent screen which, together with the inclusion of exotic species, gives the border a contemporary twist.

LEFT A magnificent clump of pampas grass points towards a view of the Middle Lake in October at Sheffield Park Garden, East Sussex. ABOVE Magnificent fountains of pampas grass illuminated in the autumn light. Pampas grass is an easy-to-grow, drought-tolerant plant which should not be overlooked, especially in areas of the country subject to hosepipe bans.

FAR LEFT Tall clumps of golden oat grass flank a path leading to the Temple Walk at The Courts, Wiltshire.
LEFT Pale sprays of Mexican feather grass combine with ruby-red sedum and other late-flowering perennials at The Courts. The autumn tones of the sumach tree glow in the background.

LEFT Translucent sprays of golden oat grass and Mexican feather grass in the White Garden at Coughton Court, Warwickshire. RIGHT Grasses in the meadow at Powis Castle, Powys, are complemented by the fiery autumnal tints of a sumach tree. FAR RIGHT Soft, feathery plumes of an oriental fountain grass contrast with the metallic blue thistles of sea holly at Lacock Abbey, Wiltshire, in September.

Autumn Colour and the Landscape Garden

The predominantly green landscape garden undergoes a transformation during autumn, as deciduous trees turn to warm shades of red and gold which, when interwoven with a thread of evergreens, forms a magnificent textural tapestry. This striking effect is magnified when reflected in an expansive lake.

To create such an impact, native trees such as oak and beech mingle with American oaks and Japanese maples, providing a rich canvas on which to showcase individual exotic specimens of tulip tree, sweet gum, tupelo and other horticultural treasures collected from around the globe. The small, round leaves of the katsura tree are a particular feature, turning a honey yellow colour in autumn and smelling deliciously of burnt caramel when crushed.

LEFT An impressionistic picture created by the reflections of autumn leaves in the lake at Lyme Park, Cheshire. **ABOVE** Autumnal colours reflected in the 2-hectare (5-acre) lake at Mount Stewart, County Down.

ABOVE Autumn leaf colour, Clockwise from top left: rich tones and a distinctive leaf shape make the Japanese maple one of the autumn highlights at Plas Newydd, Anglesey; autumn leaves of a tulip tree at Mottisfont Abbey, Hampshire; light shining through maple leaves as they turn from green to red in early autumn at Hidcote Manor Garden, Gloucestershire; sycamore leaves in autumn at Lyme Park, Cheshire.

ABOVE Mellow autumn sunshine seeps through the trees of the allée leading towards Sir John Vanbrugh's Belvedere, built in 1715, at Claremont Landscape Garden, Surrey.

Stourhead in Wiltshire, one of the country's finest eighteenth-century landscape gardens, is especially beautiful in autumn. Its rich collection of trees and shrubs includes native beech and oaks, hornbeams and chestnuts, alongside magnificent tulip trees and maples interspersed with evergreen wellingtonias and cypresses, which frame the tranquil lake at its centre. The Arcadian scene, punctuated at intervals with garden buildings including a subterranean grotto, classical temples, Gothic Cottage and Palladian stone bridge spanning the ornamental lake, is an example of art and nature harmoniously balanced.

BELOW Visitors enjoying the vibrant autumn colours on a sunny day at Stourhead, Wiltshire. **RIGHT** A glorious view of the Pantheon on a crisp autumnal day at Stourhead, mirrored in the ornamental lake.

LEFT The 'perfect' landscape view at Stourhead, Wiltshire, including the Palladian Bridge and Pantheon. It is early autumn, and colours are just turning from greens to golden hues. **ABOVE** The Gothic Cottage, Stourhead, peeping through the flaming hues of autumn colour. **ABOVE RIGHT** Emerging autumn colour in the landscape gardens at Stourhead, looking towards the Temple of Apollo.

LEFT A view of the early eighteenth-century cascade on the dam at Fountains Abbey and Studley Royal Water Garden, Yorkshire. **ABOVE** The surprising view from Anne Boleyn's Seat – a Gothic alcove built in the late eighteenth century at Fountains Abbey and Studley Royal Water Garden, but reconstructed several times. This late autumn scene looks towards the Crescent Ponds with the abbey beyond.

FAR LEFT Autumn colours,
reflected in the lake, frame
the façade of the Grange at
Biddulph Grange, Staffordshire.
LEFT A colourful Chinese temple,
the Joss House, overlooks the
autumnal Chinese Garden at
Biddulph Grange.

Sheffield Park in East Sussex provides a masterclass in vibrant autumn planting for maximum contrast. Originally belonging to the Earl of Sheffield, the estate was purchased in 1909 by Arthur Soames, a local Lincolnshire brewer, who embellished the traditional landscape garden with an overlay of the boldest autumn colours. Giant evergreen conifers juxtapose with the brilliant crimson, pink and orange foliage of scarlet oaks, Japanese maples and tupelos, through which glow luminous white birch trees and the buttery plumes of grasses. The effect is altogether bold and brilliant.

ABOVE A carpet of fallen golden leaves surrounds a gnarled old sweet chestnut tree at Sheffield Park, East Sussex.
RIGHT Mellow autumn sunlight catching the scarlet leaves of the Japanese maple by the Upper Woman's Way Pond at Sheffield Park.

ABOVE LEFT Japanese maple seed capsules at Sheffield Park, East Sussex.
ABOVE The leaves of a scarlet oak in autumn at Sheffield Park. RIGHT A view
across the lake at Sheffield Park, in October. The spectacular autumn shades of
the crimson maples contrast with chalk white birch trees and acid-green conifers.

The Productive Garden – Orchards and Kitchen Gardens

In the autumn, trees and shrubs are bursting with fruit, providing valuable food for wildlife. Bright red hawthorn berries, slate blue sloes from the blackthorn and rose hips of varying shapes sparkle amongst the rich autumn foliage. Even when the leaves have fallen, berries remain on the bare branches of the trees, in full view of the birds that feast on them throughout the lean winter months.

Cultivated fruit is as beautiful as the wild berries, whether grown as a single specimen in the garden or en masse in an orchard. Orchards attract a wide variety of wildlife, from bats to beetles, birds and butterflies. This, along with lichens, mosses and fungi, increases the biodiversity of the land, especially when the orchard is managed on organic principles. Orchards are one of the oldest forms of a garden. They were especially important in the days when cider was safer to drink than water, and every estate would have had at least one. The old cider orchards at Barrington Court, Somerset, have once again been put to use and are now producing award-winning apple juice and cider.

FAR LEFT Early autumn at Woolbeding Gardens, West Sussex: a well-ordered potager with a topiary swan is surrounded by coloured salad crops. **BELOW LEFT** Medlar fruit in the grounds of Lacock Abbey, Wiltshire, in autumn. **BELOW** The edible fruit of the flowering dogwood at Winkworth Arboretum, Surrey, in November.

LEFT Deep red cider apples of an unknown heritage variety ripe for picking at Barrington Court, Somerset. **RIGHT AND ABOVE RIGHT** Collecting apples in the orchard at Killerton, Devon.

Autumn is the traditional time to harvest produce from the kitchen garden before winter sets in. At this time of year it can be as beautiful as any other part of the garden, with bountiful squashes and pumpkins, espaliered fruit and beneficial flowers. The National Trust has an impressive array of working kitchen gardens and is restoring many more, largely to grow produce for its own cafés and restaurants, and many are run by volunteers or for local communities. Clumber Park in Nottinghamshire has a glorious walled kitchen garden dating from the 1770s and spanning 1.6 hectares (4 acres). Cultivated within its walls is a vast range of produce, including many historic varieties of fruit and vegetables, while the magnificent Edwardian glasshouses offer protection to a mouth-watering collection of fruit, including peaches and vines (see page 177). More recently, the kitchen garden at Tyntesfield in Somerset has undergone a programme of restoration and is now almost fully productive. In its Victorian heyday it would have been on show to guests of the family and as such was furnished with ornamental gates and buildings, including an Italian loggia. The glasshouses have also been restored and are once again filled with figs, peaches, vines, tomatoes and cucumbers.

LEFT Flowers and vegetables growing in the kitchen garden in early autumn at Tintinhull Garden, Somerset.
BELOW Early autumn flowers and heritage varieties of vegetables in the Kitchen Garden at Oxburgh Hall, Norfolk.

ABOVE LEFT Plums in the orchard at Lyveden New Bield, Northamptonshire, in September. **ABOVE RIGHT** Espaliered pears in September at Bateman's, East Sussex. **BELOW LEFT** Pumpkins in the Victorian Kitchen Garden at Oxburgh Hall, Norfolk. **BELOW RIGHT** Fragrant golden fruit on a quince tree in September at Peckover House and Garden, Cambridgeshire. **RIGHT** Ripe grapes hanging from the vine in one of the glasshouses at Clumber Park, Nottinghamshire.

LEFT Ruby chard growing in the kitchen garden at Tyntesfield, Somerset, in early autumn. **ABOVE** A view through a doorway into the Kitchen Garden at Tyntesfield. The garden is enhanced by colourful dahlias. **RIGHT** Crops protected by netting in the kitchen garden at Tyntesfield.

winter

Winter Gardens

As the year draws to a close, the drama of autumn gives way to the stillness of winter. Stripped of their leaves, the naked trees are unmoved by all but the strongest winds; most herbaceous plants will have retreated below ground, while the frosted stems of those that remain are brittle and unyielding. Even rippling water or gushing fountains may be arrested in mid-flow. Only the movement of a hungry bird scavenging for food disturbs the stillness, puffed up to insulate itself against the cold in the bare branches of the trees or searching for worms in empty borders.

PREVIOUS PAGE At Anglesey Abbey, Cambridgeshire, the Serpentine Walk is edged in evergreen sweet box, with the colourful stems of pollarded golden willows rising above. LEFT Icicles highlight the fountain in the Fountain Garden at Woolbeding Gardens, West Sussex. RIGHT Sheep sheltering under the magnificent snow-covered cedar of Lebanon at Woolbeding Gardens.

The calm is accentuated in the formal garden, where clipped evergreen hedges and topiary in unvarying shades of green stand motionless, their forms accentuated by a dusting of snow. Deciduous beech hedges retain their russet leaves throughout winter, injecting a warming contrast to winter's cool palette. The sculptural and architectural features of a garden take centre stage, unchallenged by summer's floral showstoppers. Winter is the season when the bones of a garden can best be appreciated.

Traditionally, this is the time of year when the garden has been put to bed. However, with more National Trust gardens now staying open all year round, there has been a move towards planting areas for winter interest. By imaginatively combining evergreen foliage, winter-flowering trees and shrubs, colourful stems and bark, and jewel-like berries, gardens in winter can be as rich in colour, texture and scent as any in summer. Anglesey Abbey in Cambridgeshire hosts the National Trust's flagship winter garden, created in 1998, while Dunham Massey, Cheshire, has the largest, covering an area of around 3 hectares (7 acres).

ABOVE Winter light filtering through the Pillar Garden at Hidcote, Gloucestershire, and illuminating a fringe of dried herbaceous stems and seed heads seen against pillars of evergreen yew. **RIGHT** The avenue of playful topiaried yews at Lytes Cary Manor, Somerset, mimics the garden's dovecote-styled water tower. In the winter the yews' elongated shadows create vivid stripes along the frosted lawn.

The Formal Garden

It is during the winter months that the strong, structural elements of a formal garden come to the fore. Crisply clipped evergreen hedges and topiary, which in summer take second fiddle to the abundant herbaceous planting within, now become the focus, providing a reassuring visual link between the garden and the house. Under a blanket of snow, clipped hedges and topiary shapes take on an altogether more billowing form, while the low winter sun casts their elongated shadows across the garden.

The formal garden at Ham House in Surrey originated in the seventeenth century along the lines of the geometric Dutch gardens. Remarkably, its layout has changed little over the centuries, making it one of the earliest and therefore rarest gardens in the care of the National Trust. Much of the planting, on the other hand, has inevitably been replaced over the years, but always with a nod to the seventeenth-century design. A tunnel of pleached hornbeams is under-planted with a low yew hedge, providing a warm russet canopy above the dark green base. Running alongside the tunnel is the Cherry or East Garden. A simple pattern of box-edged beds, with clipped box cones spaced at intervals, are filled alternately with dwarf cotton lavender 'Nana' and Dutch lavender, trimmed to pincushion mounds of evergreen foliage. Although based on a plan from 1671, the simplified use of plants in this parterre ensures that this garden maintains a contemporary feel. The central focal point is a statue of Bacchus. This garden works as well in the winter frosts as it does in the summer sun.

LEFT The hornbeam tunnel at Ham House, Surrey, is given visual stability by the dense yew hedge at the base, while retaining light above through the tracery of winter branches. BELOW Visitors enjoying the low winter sun at Ham House, as it silhouettes the geometric hedges and reveals the delicate tracery of the trees.

LEFT The Cherry or East Garden at Ham House, Surrey, in the snow.

ABOVE Detail of the topiary box cones in the Cherry or East Garden at Ham House.

LEFT AND RIGHT Tucked away behind tall,
architectural yew hedging, the formality of the
late nineteenth-century sunken Dutch Garden at
Clandon Park in Surrey is softened by a sprinkling
of snow and the shapes of the bare branches of the
trees beyond.

On a much larger scale, the topiary gardens at Chirk Castle in Wrexham are composed of massive boulders and castellated hedges to provide protection from the wind that whistles through this exposed site. Within the battlements, the terraced lawn is ordered with double rows of large cones and topiary 'Welsh hats', with a magnificent crown as a centrepiece. The pruning of the topiary takes three gardeners two months to complete, but the effort is worthwhile as it provides the garden with interest throughout the year. In winter, these dark green forms are relieved by a clear view of classical stone statues and by the tracery of deciduous trees in the park beyond, while snow settling on their flat, curiously shaped surfaces accentuates the abstract composition. The Chirk topiary was planted in the nineteenth century, but it was allowed to grow to its present exaggerated form on the advice of the influential garden designer Norah Lindsay, a friend of the tenants Lord and Lady Howard de Walden, in the early twentieth century.

LEFT A dusting of snow on the sombre dark green topiary boulders in the Formal Garden at Chirk Castle, Wrexham, highlights their curious forms.

LEFT Statues of nymphs are accentuated by the dark green backdrop of yew hedging in winter, flanking the view to the Hawk House in the distance at Chirk Castle, Wrexham. **ABOVE** Yew topiary casting long shadows in the Formal Garden at Chirk Castle. A statue of Hercules is a focal point in the distance.

RIGHT This regimented row of giant yews at The Courts Garden, Wiltshire, was originally designed to complement the formality of the main lawn. Over the years, the pillars of yew have been allowed to evolve into a more organic shape, providing an idiosyncratic sculptural contrast to the formal element of the garden. **FAR RIGHT** At The Courts, a low winter sun illuminates the textures of the brick path and lawn studded with early bulbs, all framed by low formal hedges and the arching branches of deciduous trees.

FAR LEFT A winter blanket of snow highlights the strong lines of the formal garden at Powis Castle, Powys. ABOVE A lead statue of a shepherd with his sheep on the Aviary Terrace at Powis Castle, provides a narrative as it faces out over the formal garden to the Arcadian landscape beyond. LEFT The delicate yellow flowers of winter-flowering witch hazel associate well with golden variegated ivy when seen against the dark green formal hedging at Powis Castle.

Plants with Winter Interest

Increasingly, as the National Trust is opening its gardens throughout the year, there is a requirement to extend the season of interest with regard to plants. This has opened up opportunities for many talented gardeners to create new winter gardens alongside the historical ones they already maintain.

Together with evergreens, trees and shrubs with exceptional bark colour or texture form the backbone of the winter garden. The icy white trunks and branches of the silver birch seem to exemplify winter, while a coppice of fiery red and orange willows or dogwoods adds warming flames to the winter chill. The polished coppery bark of the Tibetan cherry glows at this time of year, as effective as any sculpture. The cinnamon-coloured paperbark maple kindles an impulse to tear away the peeling layers of bark, whereas the snakebark maple has smooth, olive green bark streaked with white. The maple *Acer pennsylvanicum* has bark of a jade green colour, while its form 'Erythrocladum' is brilliantly coloured with intense, candy pink bark. The coral bark maple is equally beautiful, in a subtler coral hue. These are plants more familiar when planted as a single specimen, but seen en masse, their effect is breathtaking.

FAR LEFT The ghostly effect of a copse of Himalayan birch is evident in December at Anglesey Abbey, Cambridgeshire. **BELOW LEFT** The coppery branches of the Tibetan cherry arising from the frosted stems of dogwood 'Winter Beauty' in the Winter Garden at Anglesey Abbey. **BELOW RIGHT** On the Winter Walk at Anglesey Abbey, the peeling bark of a paperbark maple is always a talking point.

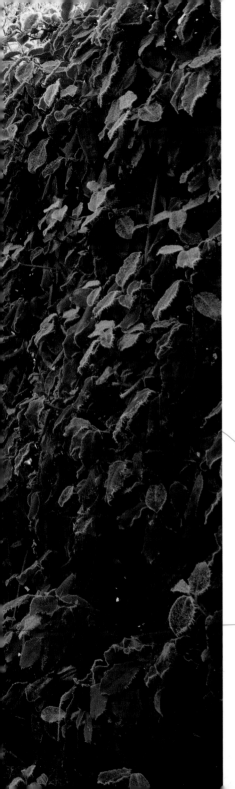

At Anglesey Abbey in Cambridgeshire, the 1998 centenary of the 1st Lord Fairhaven's birth was the catalyst for the creation of a new 1-hectare (2½-acre) winter garden. It was designed by John Sales, chief gardens advisor at the National Trust at the time, together with the then head gardener, Richard Ayres. It is planned around a Serpentine Walk, a backdrop of evergreens providing the perfect foil to show off the various colours of the plants within. Generous groupings of trees and shrubs with flamboyant coloured barks of fiery reds and oranges or ghostly whites flank the path (see pages 200–211).

LEFT This bronze statue is a memorial to Huttleston Broughton 1st Lord Fairhaven, who developed the gardens at Anglesey Abbey in the early twentieth century. ABOVE The glowing red berries of Irish yew, seen here at Anglesey Abbey.

TOP A view of the Winter Walk at Anglesey Abbey, with evergreens and the frosted stems of deciduous shrubs. **ABOVE** The Winter Walk at Anglesey Abbey, in February. The colourful stems of the dogwood 'Winter Beauty' and Siberian dogwood, and white-stemmed brambles and snowdrops, weave an interesting texture. **RIGHT** At Anglesey Abbey, the Serpentine Walk is edged with evergreen winter box, with the colourful stems of pollarded golden willows rising above.

The heady scents of the winter-flowering honeysuckle, Oregon grape, viburnum, wintersweet and sweet box pervade the air. Plants that retain their fruit into the winter are studded with berries. Some are accentuated by glossy evergreen foliage – hollies, cotoneaster and the strawberry tree; others adorn the naked branches of countryside favourites such as crab-apple trees and hawthorns. Glistening scarlet, bead-like fruits furnish the native guelder rose, while the unusual beautyberry is bedecked with clusters of tiny purple berries. Halfway along the Walk is an enclosed circular space subtly planted with a simple combination of grasses – blue fescue and creamy Mexican feather grass – frozen crisp and still in the white winter frost. A central bronze statue, a memorial to Huttleston Broughton (who was responsible for creating the gardens in the early twentieth century), provides a focus for contemplation.

In 2007, Dunham Massey in Cheshire followed suit with Britain's largest winter garden created out of a 3-hectare (7-acre) paddock, created with advice from the acclaimed plantsman Roy Lancaster. Trees and shrubs include those with remarkable bark (such as the textured snake-bark maples), brightly coloured willows and dogwoods, and pale-stemmed birches. These are planted together with winter-flowering cherries and camellias, while the small flowers of sweet box, viburnums, daphnes and wintersweet imbue the air with sweet fragrance. Evergreen foliage is supplemented with variegated varieties of holly and oleaster, which provide a constant structure throughout the year.

From January, Dunham Massey is carpeted with 250,000 or so double- and single-flowered snowdrops consisting of around 240 different varieties. Anglesey Abbey has its own particular hybrid, found in the 1960s on a rubbish tip of the Victorian garden by Richard Ayres, who also has a snowdrop named after him. These not only transform the landscape for a few weeks in late winter, but are a source of food for honey bees out foraging on mild days.

OPPOSITE, TOP Yellow wintersweet in the Winter Garden, Anglesey Abbey. Its nodding, pale yellow, starry flowers have a sweet, spicy perfume. LEFT A late cotoneaster in December at Anglesey Abbey. OPPOSITE, BOTTOM Clusters of purple berries grace the free-fruiting beautyberry 'Profusion' in December at Anglesey Abbey. BELOW The very vigorous Oregon grape 'Lionel Fortescue', with upstanding racemes of fragrant bright yellow flowers at Anglesey Abbey, in December.

ABOVE Winter-flowering beauties to look out for in the Winter Garden at Anglesey Abbey include the viburnum 'Candidissimum', a white form of the popular, deliciously scented shrub (left) and the greater snowdrop 'Galadriel' (right).

ABOVE Also in the Winter Garden are pink varieties of viburnum (left) and the pleated snowdrop 'Chequers' (right). Often with scented flowers followed by colourful fruits and with evergreen or deciduous varieties to choose from, viburnums have much to offer the winter garden.

LEFT Snowdrops sparkle beneath a grove of silver birch trees in the Winter Garden at Dunham Massey, Cheshire. **ABOVE** Iris 'Harmony' and snowdrops, also in the Winter Garden at Dunham Massey.

RIGHT Winter interest at Anglesey Abbey. Clockwise from top left: the ramrod-like branches of a dark-leaved willow; the long male catkins of *Garrya elliptica* 'James Roof', which shroud the evergreen shrub in winter; the compact *Mahonia* x *media* 'Winter Sun' and a corkscrew hazel. This curious form was discovered in Gloucestershire in 1863. The contorted stems provide an interesting winter contrast to the perpendicular catkins.

ABOVE AND RIGHT Winter interest at Dunham Massey's Winter Garden are provided by the corkscrew hazel growing in front of red-stemmed dogwood 'Siberian Pearls' (above); the invaluable winter-flowering witch hazel (right) and the iris 'Katharine Hodgkin' pushing up through the leaves of Italian arum 'Marmoratum' (opposite).

Statuary and Architectural Features

Garden architecture and statuary rise in prominence during the winter months, when herbaceous plants retreat underground for their winter dormancy. Classical temples and bridges adorn the eighteenth-century landscape parks, while oriental pagodas and pavilions are a colourful reminder of the great explorations of the nineteenth century, when architectural influences, along with newly discovered plants, were brought back by the great plant hunters of the day from all corners of the globe.

LEFT A lead statue of a bacchanalian figure in the garden at Hardwick Hall, Derbyshire. RIGHT This lead figure appears frozen in time, yet nevertheless suggests music and animation in the garden at Hardwick Hall.

LEFT AND RIGHT On a bright winter's day the honey-coloured stone of Hardwick Hall takes on an extra glow, snow highlights the architectural features of the trees and walls, and it is a truly magical place to be.

FAR LEFT The red Chinese pagoda was made for the Paris exhibition of 1867, and brought to Cliveden, Buckinghamshire, by William Waldorf Astor. In the setting of a snow-covered Water Garden, it looks particularly distinctive. **ABOVE** The columns of the Rotunda, built in 1766, are an architectural counterpart to the trees in the landscape garden at Petworth House, West Sussex. **LEFT** A snow-covered view from the Long Walk to one of the twin garden pavilions at Hidcote Manor Garden in Gloucestershire.

Intricately designed iron gates have a greater impact in the wintertime, and even a flight of stone garden steps can take on an almost abstract appearance when covered with a blanket of snow. Statuary can be used to provide a narrative in a garden, a device frequently employed in the eighteenth century. Landscape gardens such as Studley Royal Water Garden in Yorkshire, Stourhead in Wiltshire and Stowe in Buckinghamshire contain great collections of classical statuary and garden buildings. Increasingly, contemporary sculpture is being introduced to several National Trust gardens to great effect, providing a platform for living artists while giving the gardens a new perspective.

BELOW The design of the wrought-iron gate at the entrance to Nuffield Place in Oxfordshire is highlighted by a sprinkling of frost. **RIGHT** The magnificent wrought- and cast-iron Davies Gates at Chirk Castle, Wrexham, were made by the Davies brothers of Croes Foel, Bersham, in the early eighteenth century.

FAR LEFT The statue of Neptune rises from the frozen Moon Pond at Fountains Abbey and Studley Royal Water Garden, Yorkshire, in winter. ABOVE LEFT An atmospheric winter mist shrouds a statue – thought to be either Galen or Endymion – in front of the Temple of Piety at Fountains Abbey and Studley Royal. LEFT *The Wrestlers* seen in a wintery light at Fountains Abbey and Studley Royal.

ABOVE A harmonious balance between architecture and nature is suggested in this winter scene showing the Palladian Bridge over the frozen lake at Stowe, Buckinghamshire. RIGHT At Stourhead in Wiltshire, the silhouettes of the deciduous trees in the background of this winter view of the Pantheon are softened by snow.

Index

Picture Credits

National Trust Images/Rosie Barnett p.113 (bottom right); National Trust Images/Mark Bolton p19 (top right), p 20-21, p.33, p.68, p.72, p.125, p.132-133, p.134, p.135 (top and bottom), p.140, p.150, p.151, p.153 (left), p.171 (left), p.196, p.197, p.198, p.199 (top and bottom); National Trust Images/Jonathan Buckley p.5, p.10 (top), p.26, p.42, p.43 (top), p.65, p.74, p.88 (top left), p.98, p.106, p.107, p.109 (top right, bottom left and right), p.121, p.212, p.213, p.214 (top and bottom), p.215; National Trust Images/ Andrew Butler p.2-3, p.4, 8-9, p30, p.31 (top), p32, 34-35, p.37 (left), p.40, p.50 (top left), p.69 (top and bottom), p.81, p.86, p.87, p.89, p.92 (top left), p.93 (bottom right), p.95 (top right and bottom left), p.96, p.97, p.102-103, p.108, p.112, p.118, p.119 (top), p.144, p.162, p.163, p.166, p.167, p.192-193, p.194, p.195, p.223, p.224, p.225 (top and bottom); National Trust Images/Neil Campbell-Sharp p.172; National Trust Images/Brian and Nina Chapple p.115, p.136 (bottom), p.142, p.176 (bottom right), p.206 (top); National Trust Images/Colin Clarke p.220; National Trust Images/Val Corbett p.18, p.75, p.88 (top right), p.117, p.120; National Trust Images/Derek Croucher p.123, p.190, p.191; National Trust Images/Nick Daly p.175; National Trust Images/David Dixon p.27 (bottom left), p.111, p.146-147, p.169; National Trust Images/James Dobson p.153 (right), p.171 (right); National Trust Images/ Carole Drake p.174; National Trust Images/Rod Edwards p.10 (bottom), p.208 (top), p.209 (top), p.211 (top); National Trust Images/John Hammond p.222; National Trust Images/Jerry Harpur p.36, p.46-47, p.48, p.50 (top right); National Trust Images/Paul Harris p.23, p.51, p.92 (top and bottom right), p.93 (top left and right, bottom left), p.94, p.113 (bottom left), p.136 (top), p.156 (top left), p.176 (top left); National Trust Images/Ross Hoddinott p.173 (left and right); National Trust Images/Andrea Jones p.78, p.85 (top left and right, bottom right), p.100 (top and bottom left), p.104-105, p.109 (top left), p.138 (left), p.139 (left); National Trust Images/Simon Knight p.50 (bottom left), p.227; National Trust Images/ Chris Lacey p.73; National Trust Images/Andrew Lawson p.79, p.82, p.83, p.84, p.114, p.152, p.221 (bottom); National Trust Images/David Levenson p.25, p.27 (top left and right, bottom right), p.39, p.53, p.60, p.122, p.141 (top), p.149; National Trust Images/MMGI/Marianne Majerus p.22, p.50 (bottom right), p.57, p.180-181, p.200, p.201 (left and right), p.202, p.203, p.204 (top and bottom), p.205, p.206 (bottom), p.207 (top and bottom), p.208 (bottom), p.209 (bottom), p.210 (bottom), p.211 (bottom); National Trust Images/Nick Meers p.49, p.119 (bottom); National Trust Images/John Millar p.37 (right), p.62-63, p.67, p.88 (bottom left and right), p.92 (bottom left), p.95 (bottom right), p.128-129, p.186,